The BRAINY BOOK Vol. I For Girls!

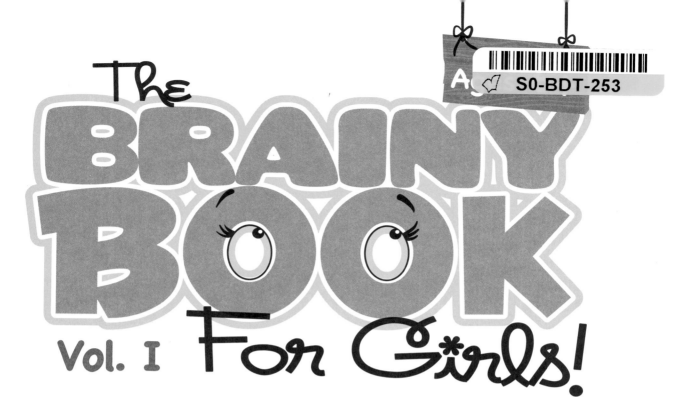

Thinking Kids™
An imprint of Carson-Dellosa Publishing LLC
P.O. Box 35665
Greensboro, NC 27425 USA

Thinking Kids™
An imprint of Carson-Dellosa Publishing LLC
P.O. Box 35665
Greensboro, NC 27425 USA

Printed in the USA • All rights reserved.   ISBN 978-1-4838-0702-7
02-082157811

Table of Contents

Table of Contents

Follow the 's to get the mermaid to the dolphin!

Start

Finish

Watching Walkers

What went wandering below?

Feelings

Look at the picture clues and use the words in the word box to complete the puzzle.

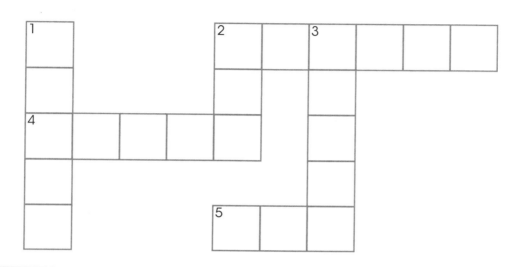

| happy | sad | shy | scared | proud | angry |

Across

2.

4.

5.

Down

1.

2.

3.

Follow the 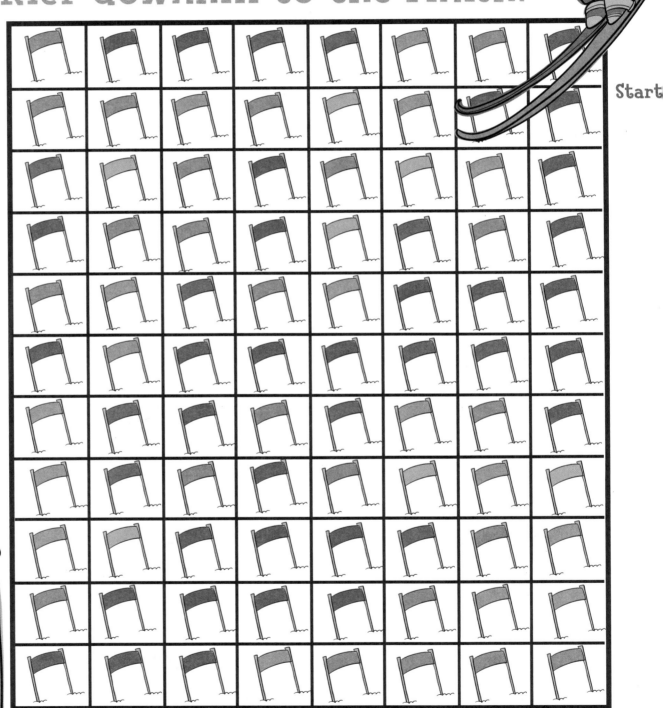's to get the skier downhill to the finish!

Start

Finish

Hairdo or Hairdon't?

Give this gal a new look!

Get a Clue!

Find and circle the words in the puzzle.

1. Tommy likes to **play** all 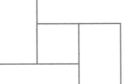 .

2. The fish got my **net** 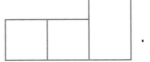 .

3. The color of her **bed** is 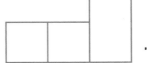 .

wet
ball
sun
toy
day
red
pie

4. Kara has **fun** in the  .

5. The **boy** had a 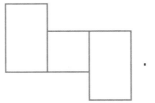 .

6. Lindsay lost her **small** blue 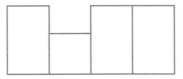 .

7. Dad's **tie** fell in his 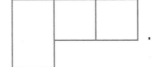 .

What's the Diff?

One of these things is not like the others.
Can you find the imposter?

Pick a Pet

Find and circle the words in the puzzle.

c	v	s	f	o	r	e	b
a	a	y	i	a	i	d	u
x	w	t	s	a	r	o	n
i	x	s	h	d	e	g	n
h	b	i	r	d	t	a	y
h	a	m	s	t	e	r	t

 cat

 bunny

 fish

 bird

 dog

 hamster

Help the cowgirl catch her cow.

Start

Finish

13

What's

Can you spot and circle the

Different?

10 differences in these two pictures?

The Pond at the Park

Read the sentences and use the words in the word box to complete the puzzle.

cattails
fish
lily pad
willow
turtle
pond

Across
4. A bullfrog sits on a _____ and croaks a loud song.
5. A family of ducks waddle into the _____ for a swim.
6. A raccoon tries to catch a _____ as it swims by.

Down
1. A _____ sits on a rock in the morning sun.
2. The weeping _____ gives shade to the animals.
3. Birds fly over the many _____ sticking out of the water.

What's the Diff?

One of these things is not like the others.
Can you find the imposter?

Things That Are Alike

Read the clues and find the other things from the word box that go with each group to complete the puzzle.

volleyball   spoon

turtle   truck

crayon   turkey

Across

1. pizza   sandwich

3. car   motorcycle

5. basketball   baseball

Down

1. dog   cat

2. knife   fork

4. pencil   marker

Watching Walkers

What went wandering below?

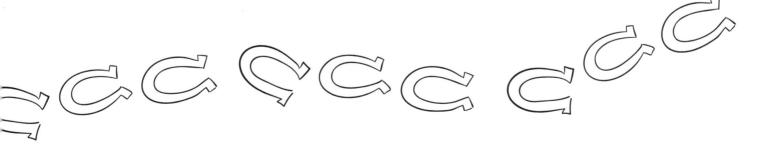

Picture Clues

Letters, numbers, and pictures take the place of words in each sentence below. Write each sentence correctly.

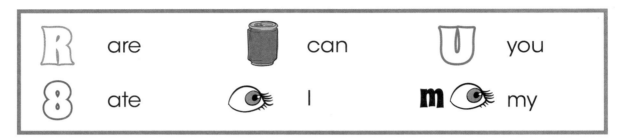

R	are	[can]	can	U	you
8	ate	[eye] I	I	m[eye]	my

1. [eye] 8 an apple.

_____

2. R U happy?

_____

3. [can] U see m[eye] dog?

_____

4. [eye] [can] see U.

_____

Summer Fun!

Fill the scrapbook with sketches of your super summer!

At the Zoo

Find and circle the words in the puzzle.

```
l  r  w  v  g  o  r  i  l  l  a  v  e
e  s  t  u  i  j  i  g  i  w  x  t  l
o  z  e  b  r  a  f  h  o  y  c  u  e
p  t  s  e  a  l  e  e  n  a  a  r  p
a  q  i  o  f  k  d  b  c  z  m  s  h
r  n  p  g  f  l  m  o  n  k  e  y  a
d  c  e  m  e  g  f  h  q  p  l  o  n
d  b  w  a  l  r  u  s  i  j  n  k  t
a  r  h  i  n  o  c  e  r  o  s  m  l
```

gorilla   camel
lion   seal
giraffe   walrus
elephant   leopard
rhinoceros   monkey
zebra   tiger

Follow the ⮕'s
to get the
piggy to the mudhole!

Start

Finish

Number This!

Unscramble and write the number words.

nnei ___ ___ ___ ___

neves ___ ___ ___ ___ ___

wetlev ___ ___ ___ ___ ___ ___

etreh ___ ___ ___ ___ ___

xis ___ ___ ___

etn ___ ___ ___

| three |
| six |
| seven |
| nine |
| ten |
| twelve |

Number This!

Unscramble and write the number words.

neo ___ ___ ___

efvi ___ ___ ___ ___

eeenlv ___ ___ ___ ___ ___ ___

wot ___ ___ ___

theig ___ ___ ___ ___ ___

rufo ___ ___ ___ ___

one
two
four
five
eight
eleven

Bakery Treasure Hunt

Find the **35** hidden items in the bakery next door.

- Ladybug
- Flower in Pot
- Ice Cream Cone
- Trash Can
- Baseball
- Log
- Butterfly
- Arrow
- Teacup
- Crescent Moon
- Banana
- Baseball Bat

- Apple
- Bell
- Crown
- Flute
- Screw
- Pear
- Lightbulb
- Pencil
- Candy Cane
- Snail
- Pushpin

- Sun
- Heart
- Lollipop
- Hat
- Shell
- Frog
- Cup with Straw
- Music Note
- Toothbrush
- Dog Bone
- Candle
- Worm

Get the girls
to the end of the
roller coaster.

Start

Finish

How's the Weather?

Find and circle the words in the puzzle.

```
s  d  b  c  l  o  u  d  y  e  a  f  w
n  h  u  r  r  i  c  a  n  e  d  c  i
o  o  a  c  s  g  r  a  i  n  y  b  n
w  t  z  x  y  t  h  i  d  e  c  b  d
y  s  v  h  w  t  o  r  n  a  d  o  y
r  c  t  u  a  k  j  r  g  f  v  a  z
f  o  g  g  y  i  h  i  m  u  l  w  x
p  l  n  o  m  l  l  j  t  y  m  n  y
q  d  s  u  n  n  y  k  s  r  q  o  p
```

sunny   tornado
stormy   hurricane
hot   hail
foggy   cloudy
windy   snowy
cold   rainy

What is your favorite
type of weather?
Draw a picture.

Crackin' Me Up!

What hatched?

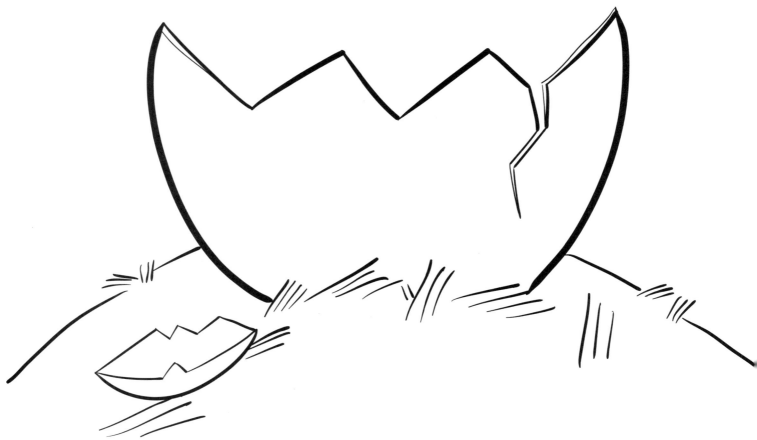

Girl Power

Find and circle the words in the puzzle.

```
t o k a p o w u w h p b m
l h a m p z o a h q t a b
e o c r i g a t a r s t o
g y a s m r o p m k c h d
g v p p s o u t d o b t y
i b e l r m r g e w o u s
n a s a c l o t h e o b u
g f a t c b o o m l t k i
s u p e r p o w e r s l t
```

cape
mask
kapow
splat
wham
boom

zap
leggings
armor
body suit
boots
super powers

Draw a picture of your
favorite girl superhero.

What's the Diff?

One of these things is not like the others.
Can you find the imposter?

Mystery Word

Write the beginning letter of each word in the boxes to make a new word.

1. | H | A | P | D |

2. | | | |

3. | | | |

4. | | | | |

5. | | | |

Write the first letter of each word you wrote to find the

mystery word. ___ ___ ___ ___ ___.

Australia

Help the **cat** make her way to the Syndney Opera House.

Start

Finish

Kitty Cats

Find and circle the words in the puzzle.

persian
siamese
maine coon
ragdoll
bengal
calico
tabby
seal point
manx

That's ME!

m	m	c	a	l	i	c	o	t	t	s
a	p	a	l	l	d	o	g	n	a	i
i	e	b	n	s	h	u	i	d	b	a
n	r	t	e	x	r	o	e	r	b	m
e	s	h	o	n	p	r	p	b	y	e
c	i	i	n	l	g	r	h	o	o	s
o	a	x	a	e	r	a	l	x	d	e
o	n	e	i	s	i	a	l	e	l	l
n	s	r	a	g	d	o	l	l	d	e

Follow the 🍎's to get the girl to the lunch table!

Start

Finish

Being a Friend

Read the clues and use the words in the word box to complete the puzzle.

Across

1. ____ the rules.
4. ____ others' feelings.
6. ____ others.

Down

2. ____ when others are talking.
3. Treat others ____.
5. ____ with others.

respect	share
fairly	follow
help	listen

Birdhouse Treasure Hunt

Find the **25** hidden items in the scene next door.

- Golf Club
- Bell
- Basketball
- Lollipop
- Pencil
- Diamond
- Open Book
- Flag
- Mushroom
- Feather
- Popsicle
- Magnifying Glass
- Grapes
- Pizza
- Caterpillar
- Leaf
- Domino
- Cane
- Cupcake
- Cherries
- Button
- Peach
- Ring
- Egg
- Sailboat

Fit for a Queen

Design your own crown.

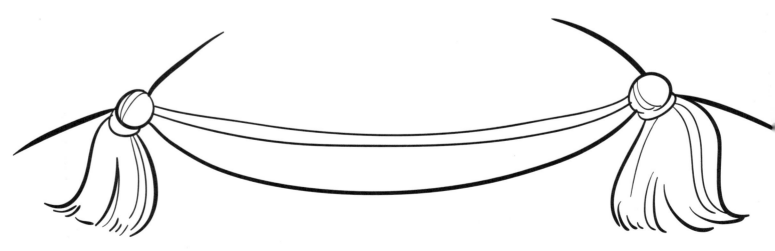

Mermaids

Find and circle the words in the puzzle.

```
s k t w c o r a l o n e s
h l l n m n i n t c s l c
i m e r m a i d u e i e a
m k h i i t a s r a x v l
m e t a l l i c b n t e e
e g a q s t a r f i s h s
r t i n s h e l l s y a z
y e l e n t h d r c n h b
i h e a d b a n d d b d c
```

mermaid
tail
shimmery
metallic
scales
shells
sand
ocean
headband
starfish
coral

Five Senses

Read the clues and use the words in the word box to complete the puzzle.

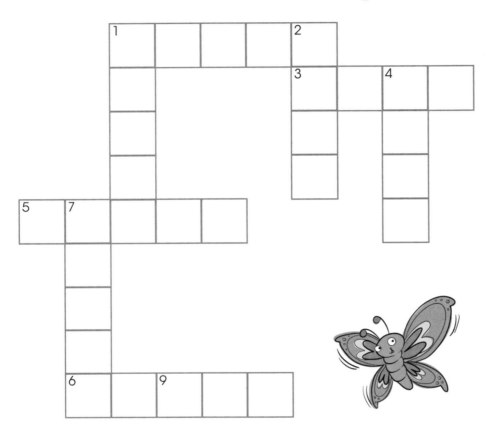

eyes
hear
ears
taste
mouth
touch
hands
smell

Across

1. Your hands help you do this.
3. You look at a pretty butterfly with these.
5. You use your nose to do this to a flower.
6. You use these to touch a soft kitten.

Down

1. Your mouth helps you do this.
2. Your ears help you do this.
4. You listen to music with these.
7. You taste your favorite fruit with this.

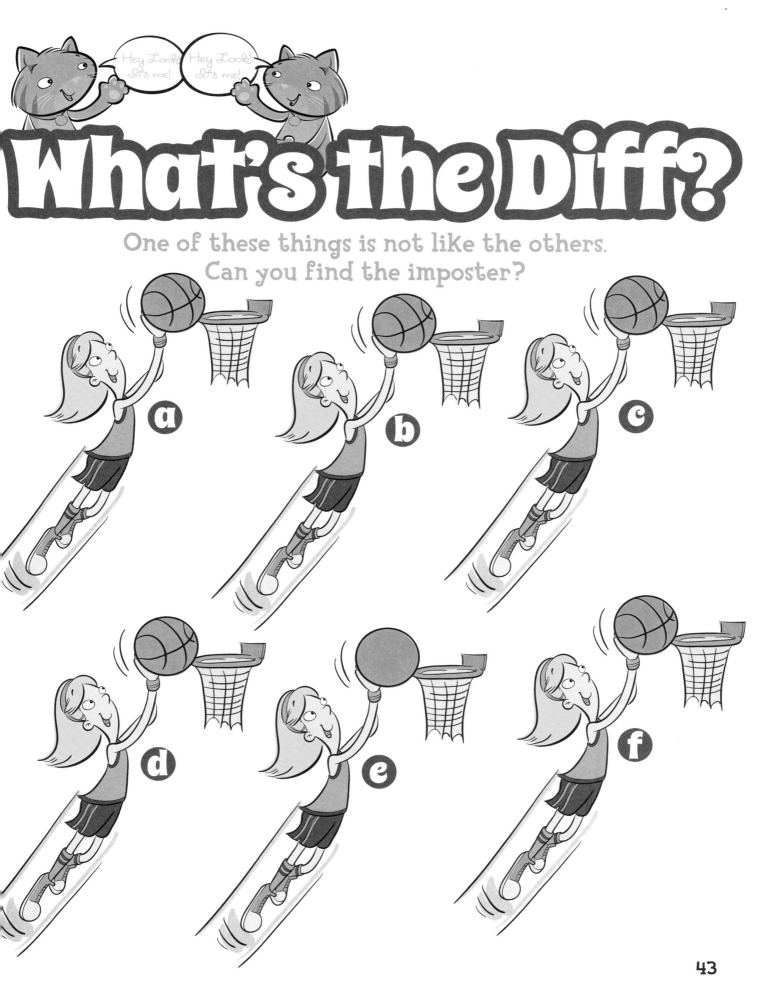

43

Secret Word

Use the clues to help you fill in the puzzles.

1. It means **large**. ◯ ___ ___

2. You can chew it. ___ ◯ ___

3. You can eat it. ◯ ___ ___

4. It can keep you cool. ___ ___ ◯

5. It can melt. ◯ ___ ___

6. You sleep in it. ___ ◯ ___

7. It keeps Earth warm. ◯ ___ ___

fan

ice

bed

nut

big

sun

gum

Find the secret word by writing the circled letters in order.

___ ___ ___ ___ ___ ___ ___.

Springtime

Read the clues and use the words in the word box to complete the puzzle.

| chick |
| shower |
| think |
| shade |
| thirteen |
| white |

Across
1. Clouds can be this color.
3. This hatches from an egg.
4. You do this with your brain.
5. It is a spray of water.

Down
2. The number after twelve.
5. You may find this under a tree.

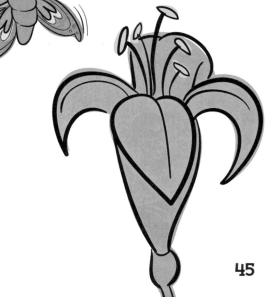

Fabulous Flowers

Find and circle the words in the puzzle.

```
d a i s y s w u t p a b s
a r p b o m a v o q r u w
f a o n l g l p u g h t e
f s q s m o p w n m l t e
o t x i e y s a n i w e t
d e r g f h e s l i g r p
i c a t c h d y o e e f e
l g a r d e n i a m a l a
e g e r a n i u m f c y y
```

rose

daisy

blossom

daffodil

poppy

sweat pea

gardenia

butterfly

geranium

lily

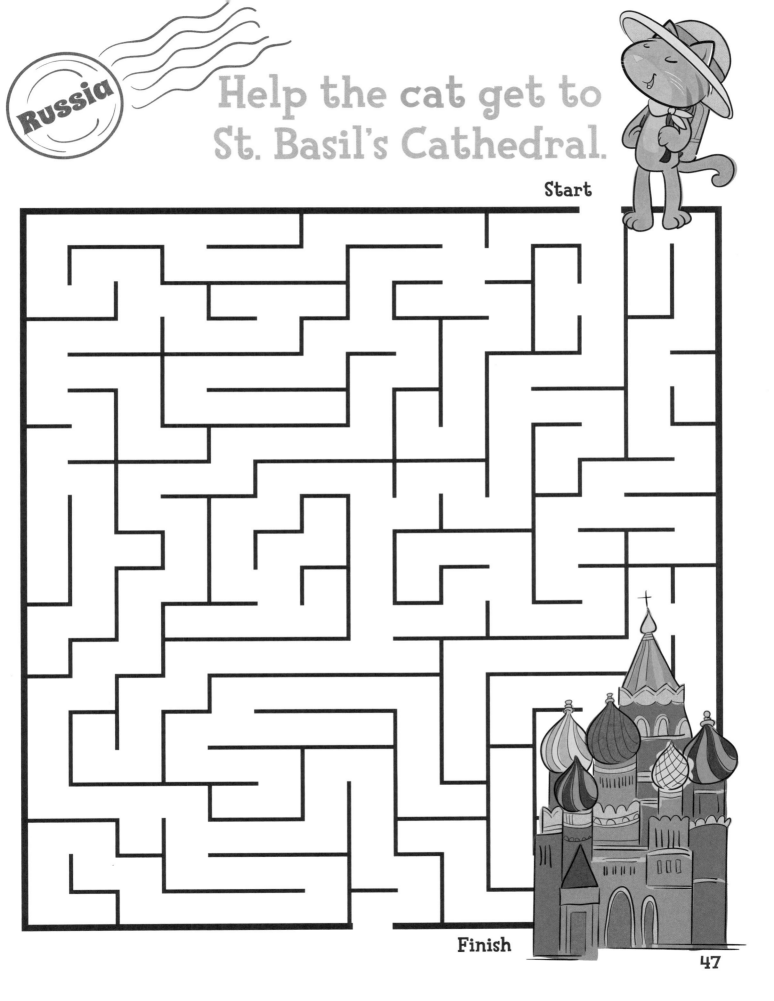

Russia

Help the cat get to
St. Basil's Cathedral.

Start

Finish

47

Weather Watch

Read the clues and use the words in the word box to complete the puzzle.

rain
thunder
tornado
cloud
storm
lightning
hurricane
fog

Across
1. This is a strong wind with rain or snow.
5. It is a very strong storm with high winds.
7. You might see a puffy white one in the sky.
8. A loud noise after a flash of lightning.

Down
2. This is drops of water falling from the clouds.
3. It is a twisting whirlwind.
4. This is a flash of electricity in the sky.
6. This is a mist close to the ground.

Baker-ME!

What kind of cake will you make?

Cupcakes

Read the clues and use the words in the word box to complete the puzzle.

```
s  f  c  t  d  e  c  a  d  e  n  t  c
p  v  r  e  n  d  e  b  c  e  v  f  h
r  a  p  o  d  c  e  h  z  d  w  h  o
i  n  e  t  s  y  b  c  k  l  i  n  c
n  i  e  o  u  t  x  s  o  i  x  o  o
k  l  o  p  g  v  i  t  j  r  d  e  l
l  l  n  c  a  c  l  n  p  e  a  i  a
e  a  a  g  r  f  s  r  g  a  r  t  t
s  t  r  a  w  b  e  r  r  y  p  s  e
```

sprinkles	sugar	vanilla	decorate
frosting	chocolate	strawberry	decadent

Bookworm

Read the clues and use the words in the word box to complete the puzzle.

title
author
illustrator
date
words
pictures
cover

Across
5. This is a person who draws the pictures.
7. This is the name of the book.
9. The writing in a book.

Down
1. The year the book was made.
2. The drawings or photos in a book.
3. The outside front and back of the book.
4. The person who wrote the book.

What's

Can you spot and circle the

Different?

10 differences in these two pictures?

Crazy Cake

Find and circle the words in the puzzle.

wheat
flour
cake
sweet
oil
sugar
cream

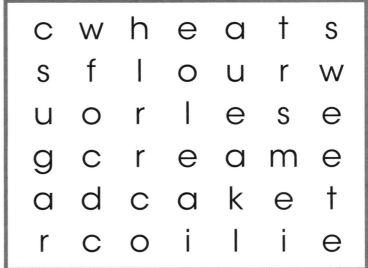

c w h e a t s
s f l o u r w
u o r l e s e
g c r e a m e
a d c a k e t
r c o i l i e

How would you decorate your birthday cake? Draw a picture.

Monsterously Tall

What is she walking?

Figure Skating Fun

Find and circle the words in the puzzle.

```
o  t  s  l  r  t  e  a  p  p
l  b  e  k  a  s  e  r  m  e
y  f  l  m  a  c  o  p  e  r
m  j  p  a  n  t  e  l  d  f
p  e  u  y  d  h  e  s  a  o
i  l  x  m  z  e  d  s  l  r
c  d  u  c  p  l  s  b  m  m
s  a  d  e  s  s  c  p  a  i
g  r  a  c  e  f  u  l  l  m
```

skates
blades
laces
jumps
graceful
olympics
medal
perform

Ballet

To find the mystery letter, color the spaces with the following letters in **blue**.

d   s   x   i   z   t   o   p   c   w   f   l   y

c	p	z	l	f
n	u	b	w	g
a	q	d	a	m
h	s	g	e	r
x	o	y	t	i

Circle the mystery letter.   **a**   **t**   **z**

At the Market

Find and circle the words in the puzzle.
Can you find an extra word?

```
a  l  k  l  i  m  p  o  s
p  e  a  c  h  e  s  a  y
h  t  o  c  s  e  l  s  e
l  r  u  e  q  t  s  o  b
a  p  p  l  e  s  h  u  r
g  x  d  a  p  o  l  p  e
p  o  p  s  i  c  l  e  a
c  h  e  e  s  e  t  k  d
```

The extra word I found is _____.

cheese	milk	peaches	apples
bread	soup	salt	

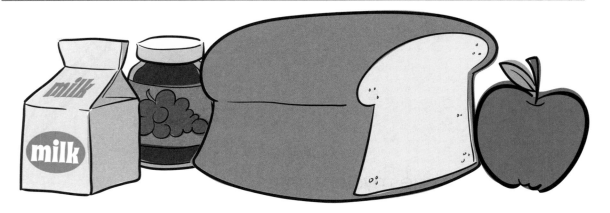

What's the Diff?

One of these things is not like the others.
Can you find the imposter?

It's a Mystery

Fill in the puzzle with the words that name the pictures below. Use the word box to help you.

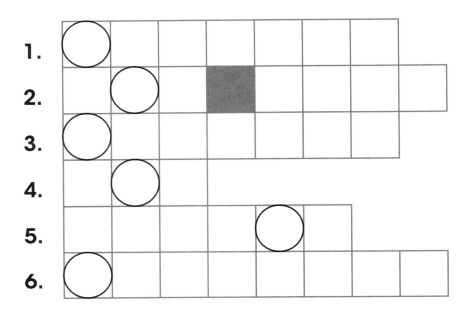

bib
bonnet
blanket
bottles
stroller
car seat

1.

2.

3.

4.

5.

6.

The letters in the circles going down the puzzle spell a mystery word. The word names people who might use all these items. Write the mystery word.

_____

Tasty Snacks

Find and circle the words in the puzzle.

```
p e p p e r m i n t
o g g r a p e s r u
p t u j k n s e a f
c v p a s q c u p c
o w e p o r o a t m
r i a p b r e a k f
n g n l b l u e b e
f h u e f r u i t c
w a t e r m e l o n
```

watermelon
popcorn
pancake
fruit
peanut
peppermint
grapes
apple

61

Butterflies

To find the mystery letter, color the spaces with the following letters yellow.

e m c q y r o j a

e	b	s	d
q	k	t	f
c	a	m	i
o	g	y	n
r	h	j	p

Circle the mystery letter.   d   h   m

Draw a picture of a butterfly.

Poodoodle!

Pretty up this posh pooch!

Carousel Treasure Hunt

Find the 35 hidden items on the ride next door.

- ❑ Sailboat
- ❑ Apple
- ❑ Heart
- ❑ Paintbrush
- ❑ Dragonfly
- ❑ Diamond
- ❑ Ice Cream Cone
- ❑ Screw
- ❑ Crescent Moon
- ❑ Snail
- ❑ Lollipop
- ❑ Watermelon
- ❑ Key
- ❑ Banana
- ❑ Toothbrush
- ❑ Paperclip
- ❑ Carrot
- ❑ Snake
- ❑ Sock
- ❑ Envelope
- ❑ Bell
- ❑ Mitten
- ❑ Pizza
- ❑ Button
- ❑ Snowman
- ❑ Donut
- ❑ Bucket
- ❑ Cane
- ❑ Flashlight
- ❑ Pencil
- ❑ Mushroom
- ❑ Leaf
- ❑ Teacup
- ❑ Flowerpot
- ❑ Crayon

Fruit Salad

Find and circle the words in the puzzle.

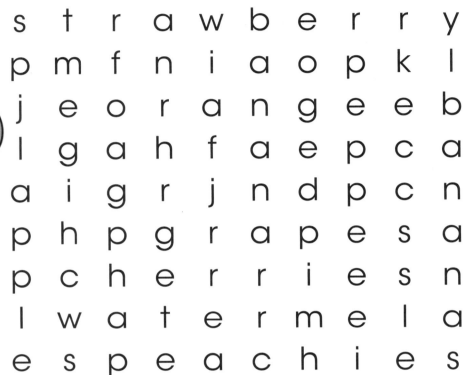

```
s  t  r  a  w  b  e  r  r  y
p  m  f  n  i  a  o  p  k  l
j  e  o  r  a  n  g  e  e  b
l  g  a  h  f  a  e  p  c  a
a  i  g  r  j  n  d  p  c  n
p  h  p  g  r  a  p  e  s  a
p  c  h  e  r  r  i  e  s  n
l  w  a  t  e  r  m  e  l  a
e  s  p  e  a  c  h  i  e  s
```

apple   strawberry
banana   peach
orange   cherries
grapes   pear

Draw a picture of your favorite fruits.

Crack the Code

Write the missing letters for each word. Use the code to help you.

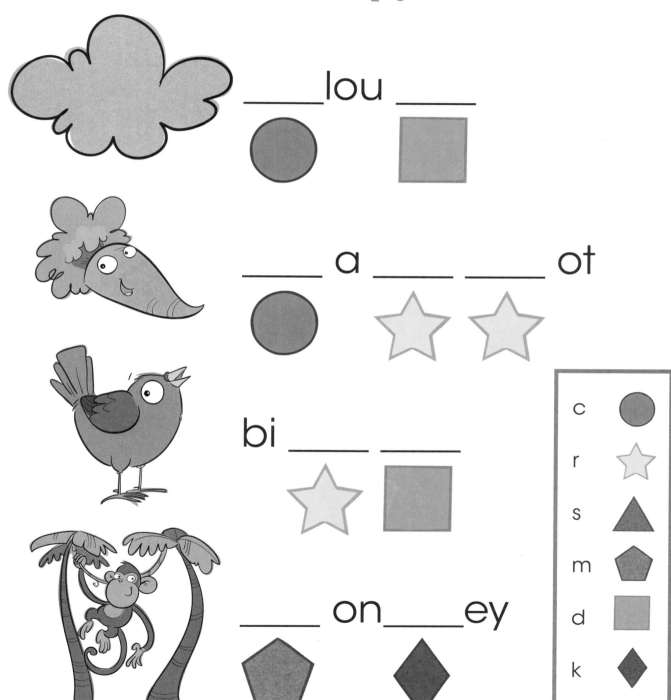

___lou ___

___ a ___ ___ ot

bi ___ ___

___ on___ey

c	●
r	☆
s	▲
m	⬟
d	▭
k	◆

Crack the Code

Write the missing letters for each word.
Use the code to help you.

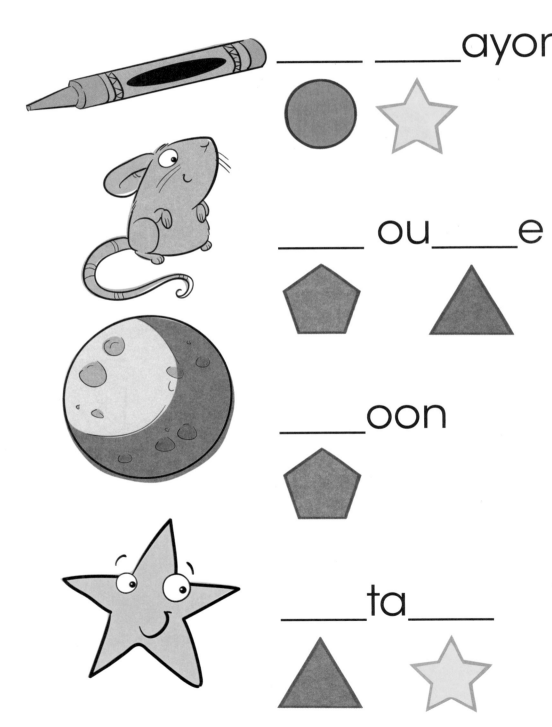

____ ____ayon

____ ou____e

____oon

____ta____

c	●
r	☆
s	▲
m	⬠
d	▢
k	◆

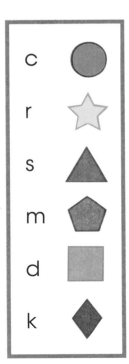

Very Veggie

Find and circle the words in the puzzle.

```
l  i  g  u  r  a  d  i  s  h  n
e  n  s  b  e  e  t  t  m  s  r
t  p  p  a  c  a  b  b  a  g  e
t  o  i  j  w  k  l  c  x  b  y
u  t  n  v  c  a  r  r  o  t  a
c  a  a  f  j  o  e  d  p  p  z
e  t  c  g  d  k  r  r  q  e  o
b  o  h  c  h  i  l  n  m  n  a
f  e  b  r  o  c  c  o  l  i  s
```

beet	spinach	potato
broccoli	radish	corn
lettuce	cabbage	carrot

I love my veggies!

69

Musical Instruments

Use the code to find out which instruments the children play.

Eric plays the $\underline{\hphantom{x}}_{11} \underline{\hphantom{x}}_{6} \underline{\hphantom{x}}_{1} \underline{\hphantom{x}}_{9} \underline{\hphantom{x}}_{10}$.

Susan plays the $\underline{\hphantom{x}}_{5} \underline{\hphantom{x}}_{15} \underline{\hphantom{x}}_{6} \underline{\hphantom{x}}_{14} \underline{\hphantom{x}}_{1} \underline{\hphantom{x}}_{12}$.

Allison prefers the $\underline{\hphantom{x}}_{16} \underline{\hphantom{x}}_{6} \underline{\hphantom{x}}_{10} \underline{\hphantom{x}}_{7} \underline{\hphantom{x}}_{6} \underline{\hphantom{x}}_{9}$.

Greg plays the $\underline{\hphantom{x}}_{3} \underline{\hphantom{x}}_{12} \underline{\hphantom{x}}_{15} \underline{\hphantom{x}}_{8} \underline{\hphantom{x}}_{13}$.

Sumi has a $\underline{\hphantom{x}}_{2} \underline{\hphantom{x}}_{4} \underline{\hphantom{x}}_{7} \underline{\hphantom{x}}_{7} \underline{\hphantom{x}}_{10}$.

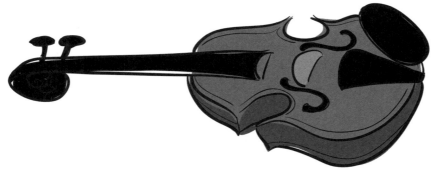

a	c	d	e	g	i	l	m	n	o	p	r	s	t	u	v
1	2	3	4	5	6	7	8	9	10	11	12	13	14	15	16

Musical Instruments

Use the code to find out which instruments the children play.

Scotty plays a ___ ___ ___ ___ ___ ___ ___ .
14 12 15 8 11 4 14

Kelsey has an ___ ___ ___ ___ ___ ___ ___ ___ ___ .
1 2 2 10 12 3 6 10 9

Nick is learning to play the ___ ___ ___ ___ ___ .
10 12 5 1 9

Howard plays the ___ ___ ___ ___ ___ ___ ___ ___ .
14 12 6 1 9 5 7 4

Annie likes to play the ___ ___ ___ ___ .
5 10 9 5

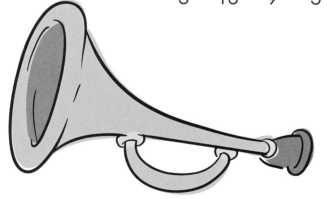

a	c	d	e	g	i	l	m	n	o	p	r	s	t	u	v
1	2	3	4	5	6	7	8	9	10	11	12	13	14	15	16

Surprise!

What would you like for a gift?

Party!

Twin Queens

Circle each letter that makes the sound you hear at the end of 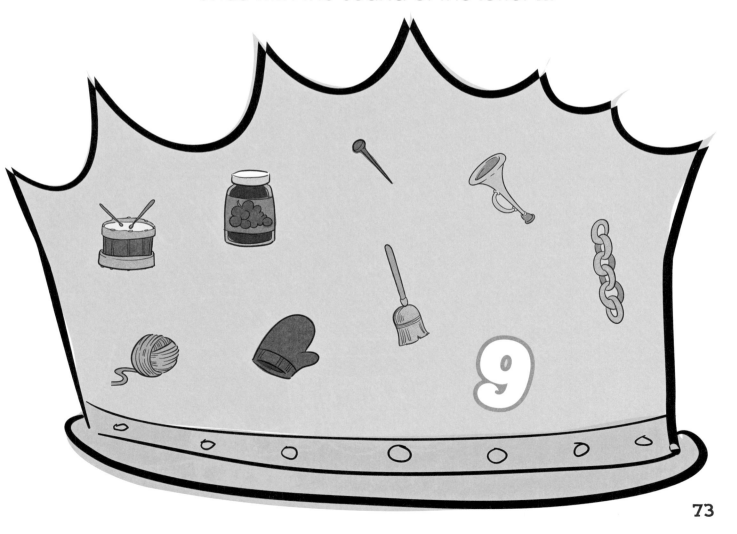 .

The queen has a grin
And a bright golden crown.
But the queen has a twin
Who wears only a frown.

Circle each picture on the crown that ends with the sound of the letter **n**.

Getting Dressed

Find and circle the words in the puzzle.

```
s  j  a  c  k  e  t  j  g  h
w  w  t  f  s  r  k  l  p  i
e  e  i  g  s  h  o  r  t  s
a  h  y  m  v  h  m  q  n  o
t  x  z  w  s  u  o  b  z  a
e  d  i  j  c  u  b  e  l  t
r  h  v  k  p  o  i  q  s  y
r  a  i  n  c  o  a  t  r  s
b  t  u  l  e  d  r  e  s  s
```

shoes   hat
raincoat   swimsuit
belt   shorts
dress
sweater
jacket

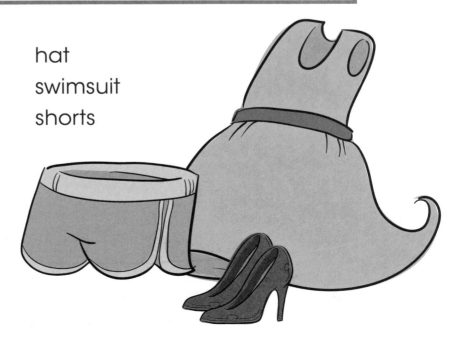

Cute Pets

Unscramble the letters. Use the pictures to help you. Then, write the words on the lines.

| a | c | t |

_____

| i | b | d | r |

_____

| s | f | h | i |

_____

| g | d | o |

_____

Draw a picture of your pet or a pet you want.

Library Treasure Hunt

Find the **29** hidden items in the library next door.

- ☐ Ice Cream Cone
- ☐ Mitten
- ☐ Ladybug
- ☐ House
- ☐ Kite
- ☐ Sailboat
- ☐ Hockey Stick
- ☐ Marker
- ☐ Comb
- ☐ Toothbrush
- ☐ Stamp
- ☐ Macaroni
- ☐ Top Hat
- ☐ Umbrella
- ☐ Baseball Hat
- ☐ Heart
- ☐ Carrot
- ☐ Music Note
- ☐ Lemon
- ☐ Trashcan
- ☐ Broom
- ☐ Soup Can
- ☐ Baseball Bat
- ☐ Ruler
- ☐ Arrow
- ☐ Teacup
- ☐ Butterfly
- ☐ Mushroom
- ☐ Apple

Help the princess find her crown.

Start

Finish

Glamorous Glasses

Add a vowel to each word below to make a new word Gladys can see through her glasses.

Gladys has some goofy glasses. They have springs on them which stretch out words to make room for more vowels.

p _ nk   p _ rpl _

fr _ me   sp _ cs

g _ _ k   c _ t _ y _

Alphabet Soup

Write the missing consonants. One has been done for you.

Nan Cook has a special way of making alphabet soup. She mixes two boxes of soup together. Then, she adds two secret ingredients—mystery and fun. After the soup is cooked, a strange thing happens. All the vowels rise to the top of the pot.

<u>s</u> o u <u>p</u>

_ o i _

_ i _

_ _ _ i _

_ o _

y u _ _ y

boil
mix
stir
hot
yummy

Everything in its Place

Each picture is missing something, and the word that tells what is missing has its letters jumbled. Unscramble the letters and write the word on the line. The first letter of each word is underlined.

| doll | grapes | canary |
| crayon | rose | beans |

1.

2.

3.

4.

5.

6.

1. pes<u>g</u>ar _____

2. ar<u>c</u>any _____

3. lo<u>d</u>l _____

4. se<u>b</u>an _____

5. eos<u>r</u> _____

6. raoy<u>c</u>n _____

Team Spirit

Design a jersey for your own team

Pucker Power

On each line, write the word that is pictured.

One day, a princess walked in the forest. She met a bullfrog who croaked loudly, "Every time you kiss me, I will turn into something different. By the seventh kiss, I will have what I need to be your prince."

_____ _____ _____ _____

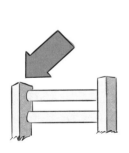

_____ _____ _____

Each word above makes a compound word when combined with the word before or after it. The last compound word tells what the frog needs to become a prince.

Write the compound words.

_____ , _____ , _____

_____ , _____ , _____

Dog Details

Use the clues to discover the order of the dogs' popularity.
Then, write each dog's name on the correct ribbon.

Clues:
- This dog is the third most popular. His name sounds like something that forms during a rainstorm.
- This dog's name includes one of man's most precious metals. It ranks fourth.
- This dog has the most vowels of all the names. It ranks second.
- This dog doesn't consider it a rotten deal to be last.
- This dog ranks first. It is as proud as a peacock.

| Golden Retriever | Cocker Spaniel | Rottweiler | Poodle | Labrador Retriever |

What's the Diff?

One of these things is not like the others.
Can you find the imposter?

Instrument Chatter

Use the word bank to help solve each riddle about musical instruments.

In my triangle-shaped body
  Many strings have I.
The notes I play
  Are from low to high.

I am a(n)_____ .

High sounds you'll hear
  When you play me.
A long tube with holes
  Is what you'll see.

I am a(n)_____ .

Strum my strings
  And sing in a band.
I play rock and roll
  In a way so grand!

I am a(n)_____ .

You'll hear a bang
  When you hit my top.
Once you hit me,
  It's hard to stop.

I am a(n)_____ .

Deep sounds you'll hear
  When you play me.
Lots of shiny, bright brass
  Is what you'll see.

I am a(n)_____ .

| guitar |
| flute |
| tuba |
| harp |
| drum |

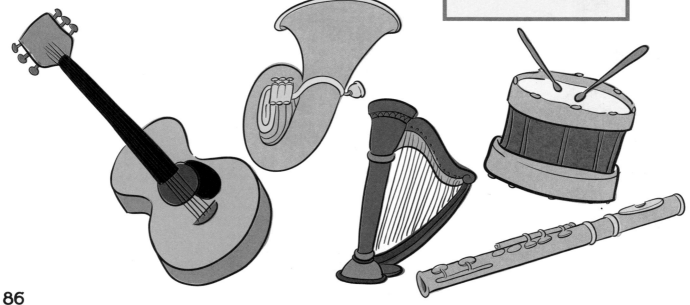

Keys to Spelling

Use the numbers on the Keys to spell out some words about music.

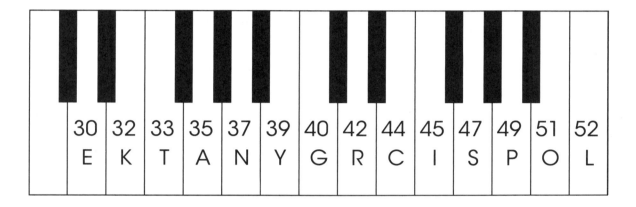

30	32	33	35	37	39	40	42	44	45	47	49	51	52
E	K	T	A	N	Y	G	R	C	I	S	P	O	L

47 51 37 40   __ __ __ __

32 30 39 47   __ __ __ __

49 45 35 37 51   __ __ __ __ __

42 30 44 45 33 35 52   __ __ __ __ __ __ __

What is your favorite type of musical instrument? Draw a picture.

What's

Can you spot and circle the

Different?

10 differences in these two pictures?

Help the
superhero
Start catch the thief.

Finish

Let Us Entertain You!

Below are five animal hand puppets. Match each puppet to its job description by writing the puppet's name on the line.

| Millie Monkey | Christy Crocodile | Ollie Octopus | Katie Kangaroo |

I am a mail carrier. It is easy for me to carry letters and packages in my own built-in mail pouch.

My name is _____.

I have a very important job. I am a firefighter. My climbing skills help me go quickly up a ladder.

My name is _____.

As a dentist I am proud of my set of perfect teeth.

My name is _____.

I am a painter. I like to paint several pictures at a time. Watercolors are my favorite.

They call me _____.

Dressing the Part

You want to act in some silly plays. Look at the title of each play below. Write the names of the costume and mask you would combine to fit the main character of each play.

Below is the inside of a costume closet.

Mouse   **Cowgirl**   **Lion**   **Princess**   **Ghost**   **Dog**

"The Invisible Woman on Her Horse" _____ _____

"The Cat Who Squeaked" _____ _____

"Her Royal Highness Barks up the Wrong Tree"

_____ _____

Rock On!

Give this gal a guitar!

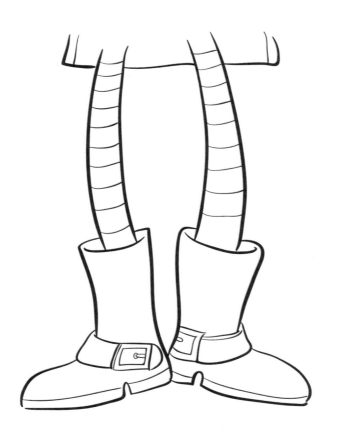

Kingdom of Sweets

Choose from the word bank names of sweet treats you might enjoy in the "Kingdom of Sweets," and write them on the sign in front of the kingdom. Cross out the foods listed in the word bank that you probably wouldn't find in the kingdom.

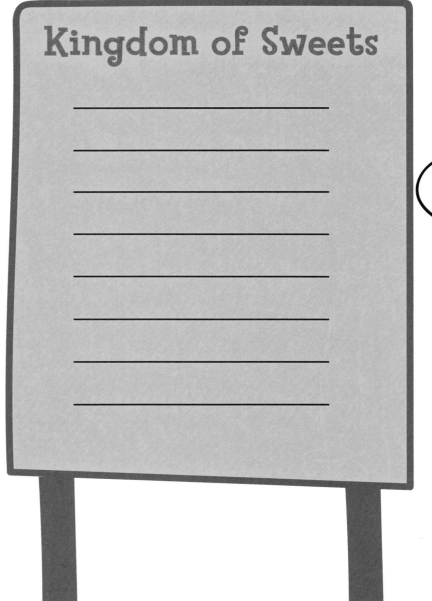

Kingdom of Sweets

_____

_____

_____

_____

_____

_____

_____

I'm the Candy Queen!

pie
beets
sugar cubes
potatoes
cotton candy
gum drops
soup
cake
lollipops
candy canes
ice cream

A Rhyme at a Time

Some poetry rhymes. Each set of two lines ends with words that rhyme.

Example: Goodness, I would like to be
Nobody else, but just me.

Finish each of these short poems by selecting and writing a word from the word bank that makes sense and also continues the rhyme.

1. I can't decide what to say,
   And yet I talk all the _____ .

2. One, two, three, four,
   Please, may I have some_____ ?

3. I can't swim outside in the winter;
   I can't go sledding in spring;
   But when autumn comes in September,
   I can hear the school bells_____ .

4. The wind is blowing through the tree,
   Waving its branches for all to_____ .
   The leaves are dragging one by one
   Playing in them in fall can be_____ .

Now, try to create your own 2- or 4-line rhyme.

tee	see
kite	sing
more	day
best	fun
tore	may
nest	ring
me	we
son	run

_____

_____

Help the **monkey** get to the big banana.

Start

Finish

Floral Fun

Find and circle the names of the flowers hidden in the garden word search.

```
A S Y E H S F D E A B U
R M L G Y I N G K J L H
T O I C A R N A T I O N
E B L E C N M R P R R F
S A R R I S M D U D C S
O L E C N R F E L V H D
R Q G H T O I N Z R I A
M C I J H A E S L U D H
I A T R F N T A G S T L
R B B D W P S R Y I E I
P E T U N I A S A O R A
```

petunia

orchid

primrose

tigerlily

carnation

iris

Take a Seat!

The conductor has the unfinished seating arrangement below. Use the clues to write in the names of the missing sections.

Clues: • The **percussion** section is directly in front of the **conductor** but as far back as possible.

• The **French horns** are directly in front of the **trombones** and behind the **oboes.**

• The remaining **woodwinds** (**flutes** and **clarinets**) are between the **oboes** and the **violas** with the **flutes** closest to the conductor.

• The **violins** occupy the largest section in the orchestra.

• The largest **stringed instruments** are in a back corner.

• The remaining **brass instruments** occupy the last section.

clarinets	basses
violins	french horns
percussion	oboes
flutes	trumpets

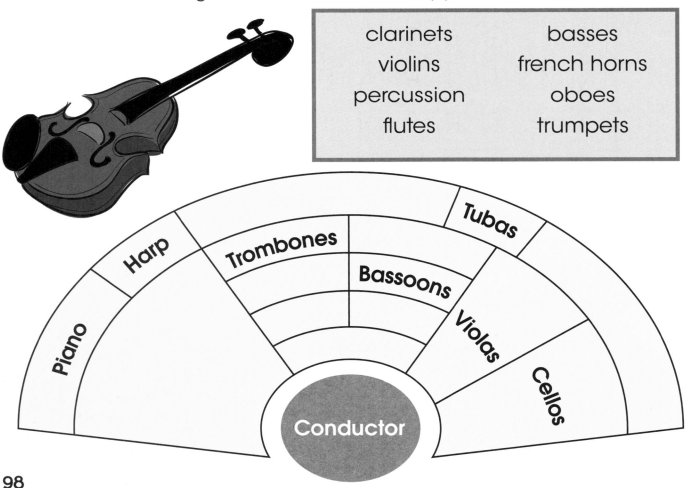

Something Fishy

Who's floating in this bowl?

Playground Treasure Hunt

Find the **25** hidden items on the playground next door.

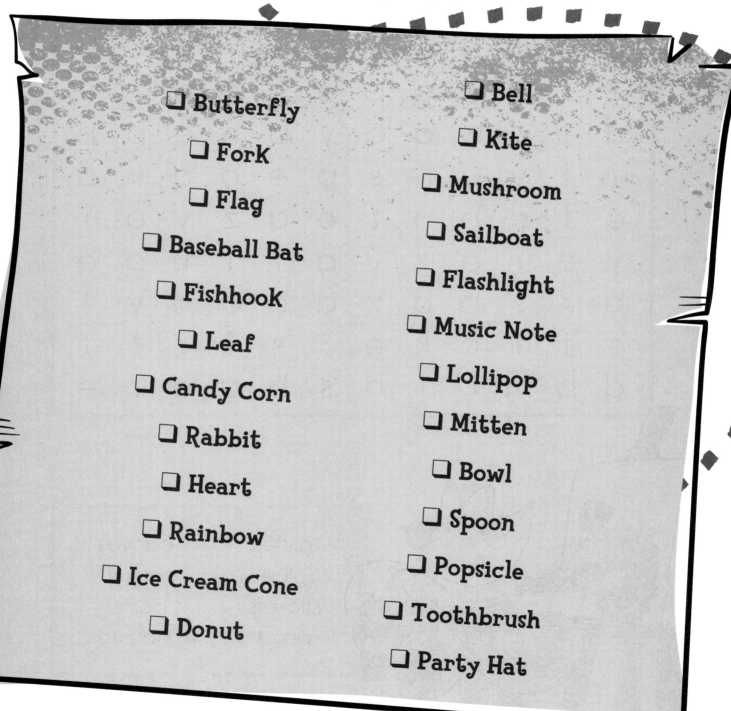

- ☐ Butterfly
- ☐ Fork
- ☐ Flag
- ☐ Baseball Bat
- ☐ Fishhook
- ☐ Leaf
- ☐ Candy Corn
- ☐ Rabbit
- ☐ Heart
- ☐ Rainbow
- ☐ Ice Cream Cone
- ☐ Donut
- ☐ Bell
- ☐ Kite
- ☐ Mushroom
- ☐ Sailboat
- ☐ Flashlight
- ☐ Music Note
- ☐ Lollipop
- ☐ Mitten
- ☐ Bowl
- ☐ Spoon
- ☐ Popsicle
- ☐ Toothbrush
- ☐ Party Hat

Get Creative

Find and circle the words in the puzzle.

```
p g l u e z l a m n o b
t l l e a p o s t e r s
u i c w a q y b n e p p
m t y a i s p e o a k a
a t e b n r e a z y a l
y e r a z v a l i k a e
b r s b b x a o d n y t
s t i c k e r s i r t t
d b m k j h s b u e r e
```

glitter   canvas
glue   easel
stickers   poster
paint   palette

102

One Becomes Two

Think of a word that could be the last part of one compound word and the first part of a different compound word. Write the missing word to make two different compound words.

pea _____ cracker

cat _____ bowl

sun _____ pot

sea _____ fish

cook _____ worm

bob _____ tail

doll _____ fly

bird _____ tub

cat	nut	flower	shell
book	fish	bath	house

Think of another compound word and draw a picture for it.

Help the monster find her way back to her closet home.

Start

Finish

Alike but Different

Write titles for these paintings. The first one has been done for you. Then, draw your own painting and write a title for it.

a hare with hair

_____

_____

_____

_____

_____

_____

IN? OR OUT?

Finish this diva's red carpet gown.

Nursery Rhyme Gifts

Each of the gift boxes below contains a useful thing for one of the characters in the listed nursery rhymes. Write the name of each present next to the name of the character to whom you would give it.

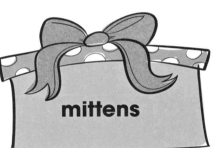

Jack and Jill _____

Humpty Dumpty _____

Little Miss Muffet _____

Old Mother Hubbard _____

Three Little Kittens _____

A Taste of Italy

Unscramble the letters to spell three different toppings on each pizza.

onpepiper

mah

oomsshmur

_____

_____

_____

mushrooms
green peppers
ground beef
ham
sausage
onions
olives
spinach
pepperoni

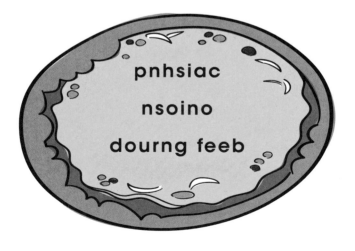

pnhsiac

nsoino

dourng feeb

_____

_____

_____

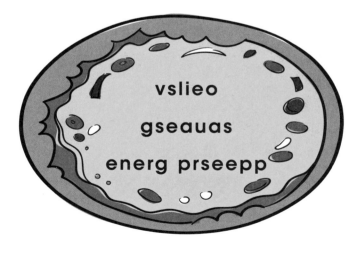

vslieo

gseauas

energ prseepp

_____

_____

_____

What's the Diff?

One of these things is not like the others.
Can you find the imposter?

Kaleidoscope of Letters

Each of the pieces of glass in this Kaleidoscope contains a letter. These letters can spell a number of valuable treasures. How many treasures can you form using only letters that are attached to each other by the sides of their triangular shapes? List them on the lines below.

_____ , _____ ,

_____ , _____

Bits and Pieces

Write the name of the story on the line.
Choose the names from the word bank.

_____

_____   _____

| Cinderella | Three Little Pigs |
| Wizard of Oz | Hansel and Gretel |

What's

Can you spot and circle the

Different?

10 differences in these two pictures?

Help the pup fetch her ball.

Start

Finish

Make Mobiles

Each mobile below needs related items to hang from each string. Choose things from the word bank that fit together. Write their names at the end of each string in their mobile.

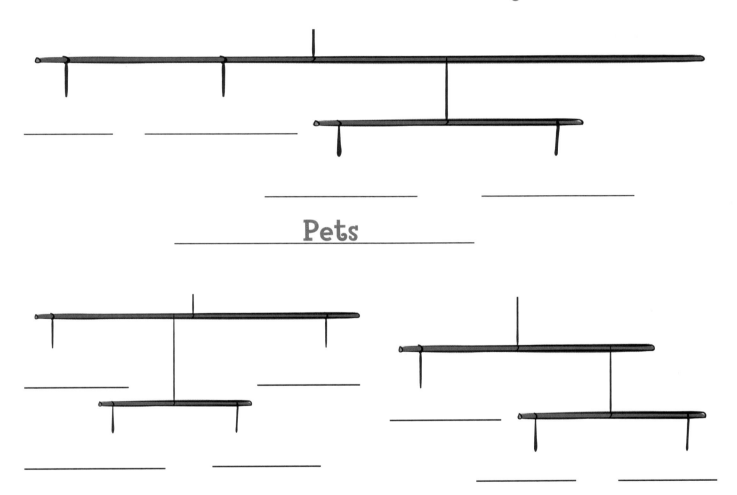

Pets

Imaginary Things   Things in Water

fairy	gnome	sailboat
leprechaun	cat	starfish
goldfish	dog	hamster
unicorn	fish	

Sew This!

Find and circle the words in the puzzle.

```
k  t  h  i  m  b  l  e  h
t  h  s  w  z  c  z  m  j
b  u  t  t  o  n  i  n  t
x  a  i  b  d  e  p  e  h
m  t  t  v  p  y  p  e  r
m  a  c  h  i  n  e  d  e
n  p  h  r  n  s  r  l  a
t  e  r  n  b  d  f  e  d
```

pin	thread	zipper
tape	stitch	button
needle	thimble	machine

Dig Her!

What is she going to find?

What's the Diff?

One of these things is not like the others.
Can you find the imposter?

118

Sweet Spring

Read the clues and use the words in the word box to complete the puzzle.

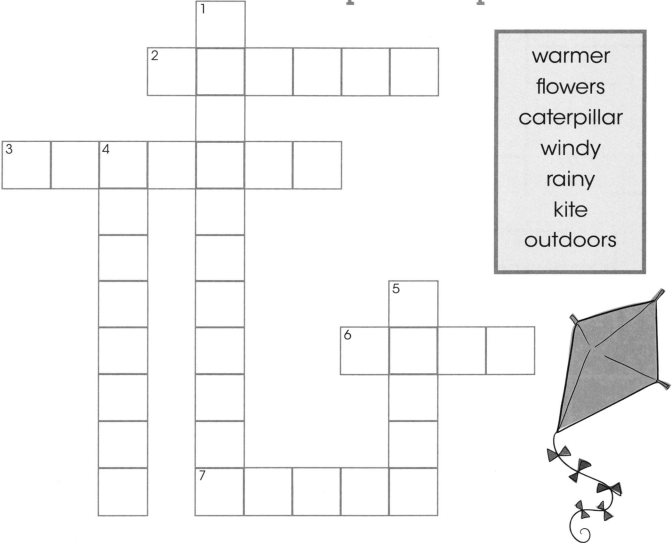

Word Box:
- warmer
- flowers
- caterpillar
- windy
- rainy
- kite
- outdoors

Across

2. It is the opposite of **colder**.

3. These bloom in the spring.

6. You can fly one outdoors in the spring.

7. Take your umbrella on days like this.

Down

1. This is busy eating new leaves in spring.

4. It's fun to play here.

5. This is a good day to fly a kite.

Help the cat visit the Colosseum.

Italy

Start

Finish

Riddle This!

Read each riddle. Then, write the answer. Use the words in the word box to help you.

play	style
babysit	nail polish
shop	

Girls do this with dolls. ___ ___ ___ ___

You go to the mall to do this. ___ ___ ___ ___

This is used for a manicure. ___ ___ ___ ___

___ ___ ___ ___ ___ ___

You can do this to your hair. ___ ___ ___ ___ ___

You earn money by doing this for younger kids.

___ ___ ___ ___ ___ ___ ___

Scream Queen!

What scared her?

Get Crafty

Find and circle the words in the puzzle.

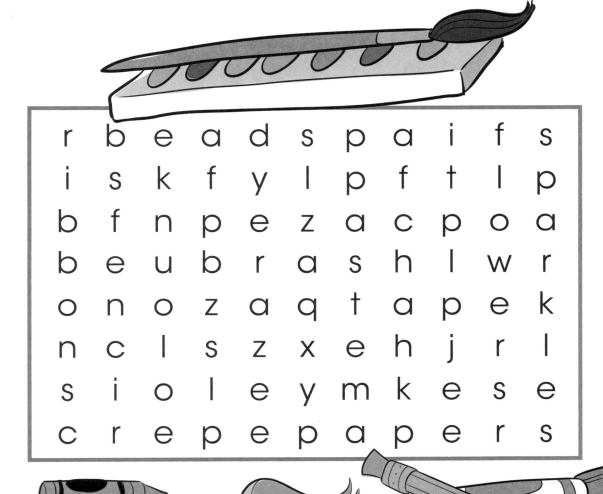

```
r  b  e  a  d  s  p  a  i  f  s
i  s  k  f  y  l  p  f  t  l  p
b  f  n  p  e  z  a  c  p  o  a
b  e  u  b  r  a  s  h  l  w  r
o  n  o  z  a  q  t  a  p  e  k
n  c  l  s  z  x  e  h  j  r  l
s  i  o  l  e  y  m  k  e  s  e
c  r  e  p  e  p  a  p  e  r  s
```

beads   sparkles   fuzzy
ribbons   flowers   feather
crepe paper

Tea Time Treasure Hunt

Find the **24** hidden items at the party next door.

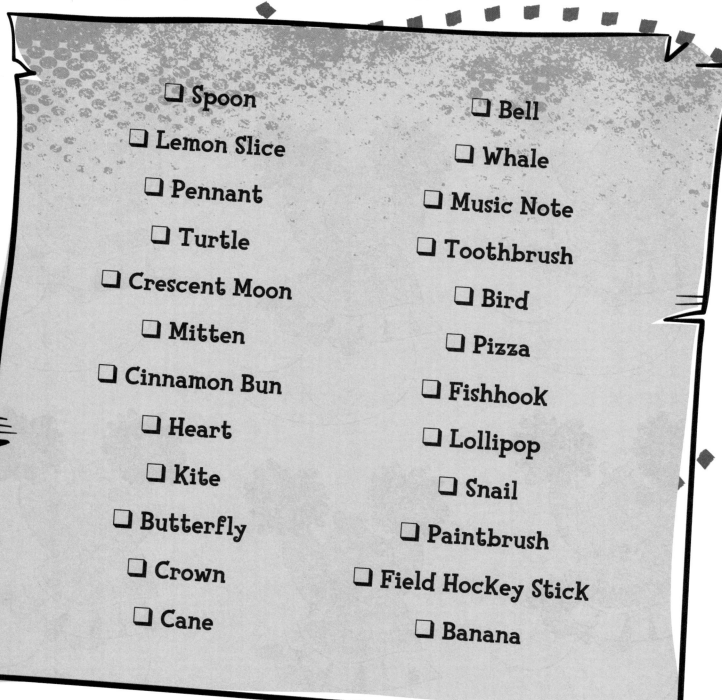

- Spoon
- Lemon Slice
- Pennant
- Turtle
- Crescent Moon
- Mitten
- Cinnamon Bun
- Heart
- Kite
- Butterfly
- Crown
- Cane

- Bell
- Whale
- Music Note
- Toothbrush
- Bird
- Pizza
- Fishhook
- Lollipop
- Snail
- Paintbrush
- Field Hockey Stick
- Banana

What's the Diff?

One of these things is not like the others.
Can you find the imposter?

Moving to Music

Read the clues and use the words in the word box to complete the puzzle.

stretch	step
dance	skip
leap	whirl
glide	pose

Across
2. This is another word for **walk**.
6. You turn fast when you do this.
7. It is a jump.
8. You do this when you move to music.

Down
1. Reach out and make your body fill more space.
2. You do this when you move with little leaps.
3. You do this when you stand very still.
4. This means **moving smoothly**.

Help the **cookies** race to the milk.

Start

Finish

Making Music

Read the clues and use the words in the word box to complete the puzzle.

Word Box

drum
horn
violin
piano
guitar
note
music
listen

Across

3. This instrument has black and white keys.
5. It is a musical sound.
6. You blow into this instrument.
7. Strike this instrument to make sounds.

Down

1. You play the strings on this instrument with a bow.
2. People do this when they hear music.
4. An electric one is used for rock and roll.
8. It is another word for **beautiful sounds**.

What's Up?

Doodle what you think is growing.

Fancy Flowers

Find and circle the words in the puzzle.

```
m  l  l  i  l  y  a  v  i  o  l
a  o  j  k  i  r  i  s  d  c  b
l  t  i  h  f  f  e  n  b  w  y
s  u  n  f  l  o  w  e  r  x  t
b  s  c  g  o  d  d  a  i  s  y
r  v  s  r  p  q  n  o  y  l  m
u  o  t  m  a  r  i  g  o  l  d
f  h  s  d  a  f  f  o  d  i  l
e  g  d  e  c  t  u  l  i  p  i
```

rose	tulip	iris
sunflower	daisy	lotus
marigold	lily	daffodil

What's the Diff?

One of these things is not like the others.
Can you find the imposter?

Fun Foods

Write each word in the correct place.

popcorn   ice cream   lollipop
candy   cookie   cake

Cheering Treasure Hunt

Find the **24** hidden items at the game next door.

- Jalapeño Pepper
- Peach
- Baseball Hat
- Broom
- Palm Tree
- Mailbox
- Party Hat
- Pushpin
- Lampshade
- Pencil
- Bean
- Leaf
- Teepee
- Slice of Bread
- Heart
- Grapes
- Teacup
- Rabbit
- Sock
- Diamond
- Carrot
- Shovel
- Pennant
- Butterfly

Help the girls untangle their jumprope.

Start

Finish

Facing the Sun

Read the clues and use the words in the word box to complete the puzzle.

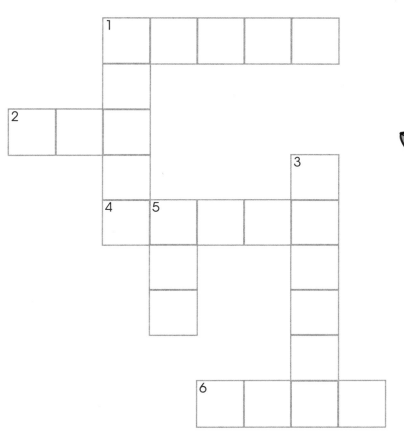

bee

cheese

eat

sheep

peach

tree

sleep

Across
1. A farm animal.
2. A buzzing bug.
4. A fruit.
6. A very tall plant.

Down
1. At night you _____.
3. A mouse eats _____.
5. You _____ food.

Finish the poster!

Soooo....Cozy

Read the clues and use the words in the word box to complete the puzzle.

bones	stove
boat	home
open	road
hole	notes

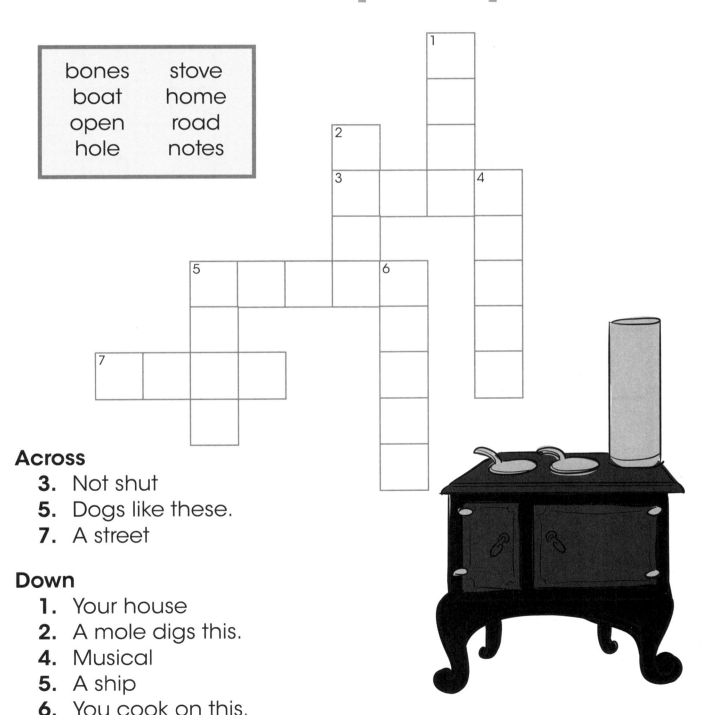

Across
- **3.** Not shut
- **5.** Dogs like these.
- **7.** A street

Down
- **1.** Your house
- **2.** A mole digs this.
- **4.** Musical
- **5.** A ship
- **6.** You cook on this.

Help the cat make her way to the Golden Gate Bridge

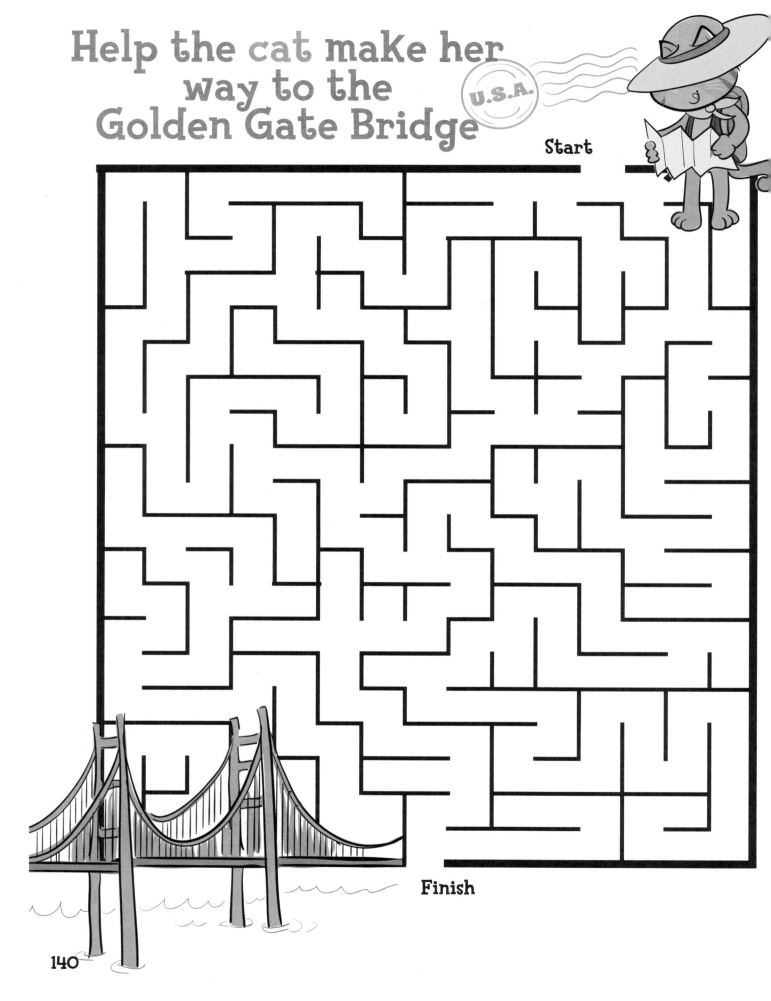

U.S.A.

Start

Finish

Summer Fun

Read the clues and use the words in the word box to complete the puzzle.

Across

2. These buzz around flowers.
3. It is the opposite of **cold**.
4. You might hear them chirp and sing.
6. Bring your lunch outside for this.
7. This kind of day is good for playing outside.

green
birds
butterflies
bees
hot
sunny
swim
picnic

Down

1. Leaves and grass are this color.
2. They flutter their colorful wings.
5. This feels good to do on a hot summer day.

Slide the ice skater to the hot chocolate.

Start

Finish

142

For the Birds

Write the bird names from the word box in the puzzle.

1. _ | a | _
2.
3. _ | _ | g | _
4.
5. _ | _ | _ | t | _
6. o | _ | _ | _ | _
7. _ | _ | e | _ | _
8. b | _ | _ | _ | _

buzzard   ostrich   eagle
jay   robin   owl
pigeons   parrots

Splashy Treasure Hunt

Find the **25** hidden items in the pool next door.

- ☐ Spoon
- ☐ Mushroom
- ☐ Candy Cane
- ☐ Chicken Leg
- ☐ Mug
- ☐ Sock
- ☐ Fishhook
- ☐ Teacup
- ☐ Mitten
- ☐ Heart
- ☐ Ladybug
- ☐ Lemon Slice

- ☐ Crescent Moon
- ☐ Baseball Bat
- ☐ Paint Can
- ☐ Rabbit
- ☐ Bowl
- ☐ Sun
- ☐ Rainbow
- ☐ Lollipop
- ☐ Leaf
- ☐ Cloud
- ☐ Light Bulb
- ☐ Egg
- ☐ Pine Tree

Marchvember 42, 4022

Toastortania, North Idohiovania

EXTRA!

Princess Pigs Out!

Art Class

Read the clues and use the words in the word box to complete the puzzle.

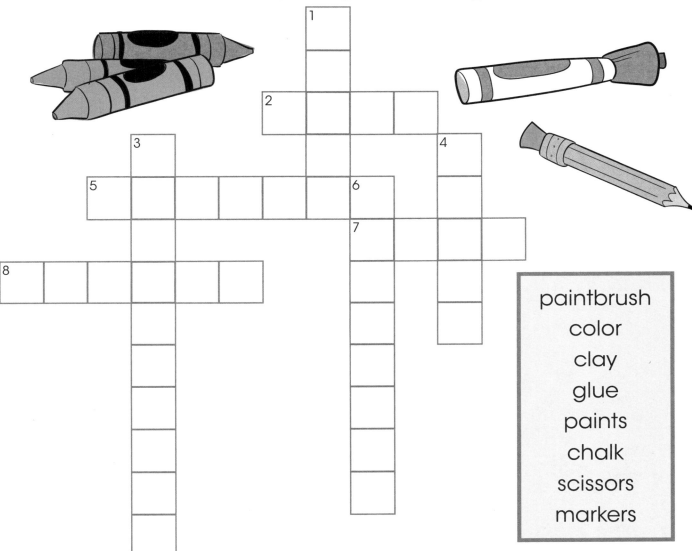

paintbrush
color
clay
glue
paints
chalk
scissors
markers

Across
2. Use this to make paper stick together.
5. Remember to put the caps back on these.
7. Make a pot with this.
8. Use your brushes with these.

Down
1. Purple is one.
3. Use this to spread paint on paper.
4. Make sidewalk drawings with this.
6. Use this to cut scraps for a picture.

What's

Can you spot and circle the

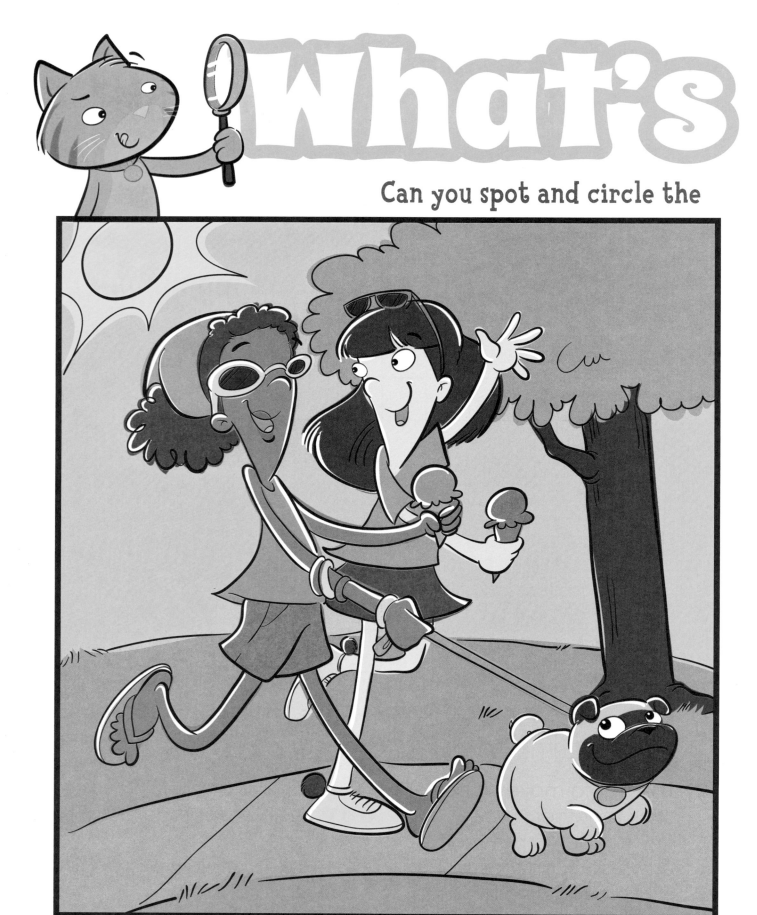

Different?

10 differences in these two pictures?

Get the forward to the empty net.

Finish

Start

Compound Fun

Match each word in the word box with a word in the puzzle to make a new word.

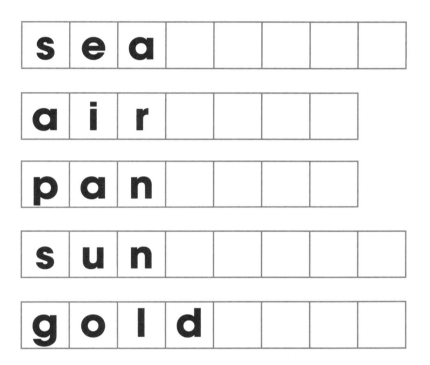

| s | e | a | | | | |

| a | i | r | | | | |

| p | a | n | | | | |

| s | u | n | | | | |

| g | o | l | d | | | |

cake
port
shine
shore
fish

Finish the poster!

WANTED

Fanny Pearl the Cow Cowgirl

DRAW 'EM SO'S WE KNOWS 'EM

Calendar Clues

Read the clues and use the words in the word box to complete the puzzle.

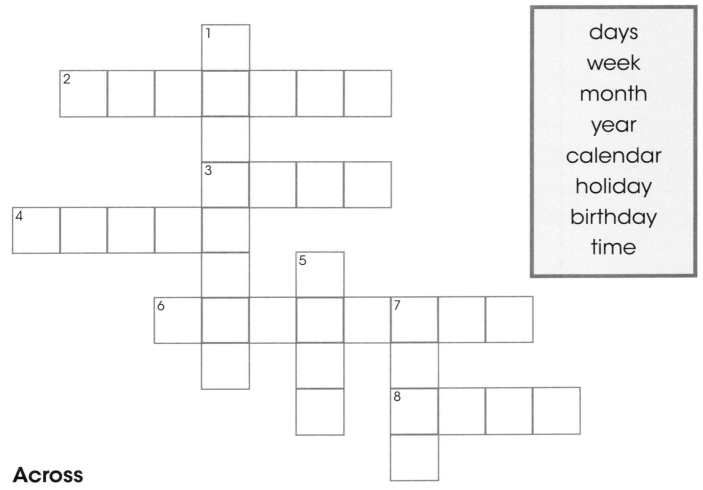

days
week
month
year
calendar
holiday
birthday
time

Across

2. It is a day for celebrating instead of working.

3. It can be measured in days, weeks, months, and years.

4. It can have 28 to 31 days.

6. You can hang it on a wall to keep track of the days.

8. This has twelve months.

Down

1. This is the day you were born.

5. It has seven days.

7. A year has 365 of these.

Gymnastics Time!

Find and circle the words in the puzzle.

```
F H I G H B A R S
L G Z U R E T C O
E M R I V T I A M
X X V I M P A R E
I E L T P I H T R
B A L A N C E W S
I M K C H C Z H A
L C O E T S D E U
I P L Q C E S E L
T E U A M N N L T
Y Y R A I T U L R
```

FLEXIBILITY   GRIP
BALANCE   HIGH BAR
CARTWHEEL   SOMERSAULT

Birds of a Feather

Draw some bodies for these bird brains!

What's the Diff?

One of these things is not like the others.
Can you find the imposter?

Help Mimi and Fifi find their way to the Effiel Tower.

oolala!

Start

Finish

Snorkel Treasure Hunt

Find the **25** hidden items underwater next door.

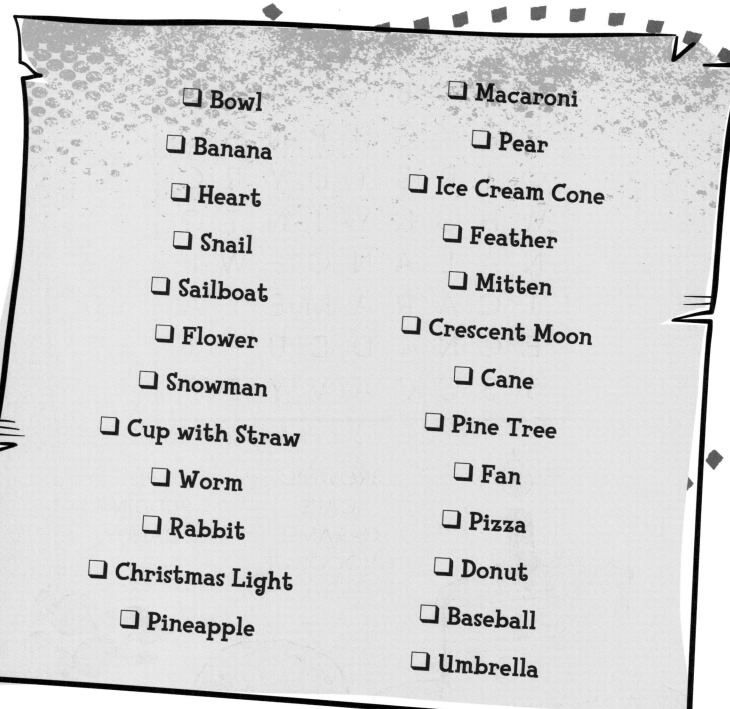

- ☐ Bowl
- ☐ Banana
- ☐ Heart
- ☐ Snail
- ☐ Sailboat
- ☐ Flower
- ☐ Snowman
- ☐ Cup with Straw
- ☐ Worm
- ☐ Rabbit
- ☐ Christmas Light
- ☐ Pineapple
- ☐ Macaroni
- ☐ Pear
- ☐ Ice Cream Cone
- ☐ Feather
- ☐ Mitten
- ☐ Crescent Moon
- ☐ Cane
- ☐ Pine Tree
- ☐ Fan
- ☐ Pizza
- ☐ Donut
- ☐ Baseball
- ☐ Umbrella

Birthday Treats!

Find and circle the words in the puzzle.

```
C I P I E M R G C
B A C B V L A A H
R J K G H P N A O
O I R E T D Y R C
W H O N Y I N T O
N A L A N C E W L
I C A R A M E L A
E G N I D D U P T
S B C O A V Y E E
```

BROWNIES
CAKE
CARAMEL
CHOCOLATE

PIE
PUDDING
CANDY

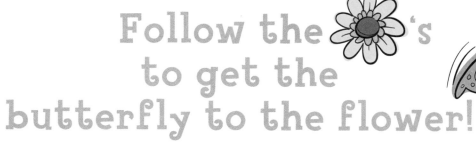

Follow the 🌼's to get the butterfly to the flower!

Start

Finish

Crafty Tools

Find and circle the words in the puzzle.

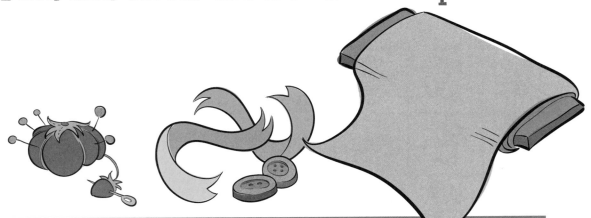

```
T  L  C  Z  F  W  K  T  X  R  M  R
U  H  H  I  T  O  D  O  H  Y  S  I
B  X  R  A  R  N  O  E  O  P  T  B
S  U  P  E  E  B  R  T  A  H  I  B
B  E  T  E  A  U  A  T  L  L  T  O
S  U  D  T  S  D  T  F  A  H  C  N
Q  L  H  A  O  E  Y  D  P  I  H  J
E  N  E  D  R  N  E  E  N  S  M  S
F  M  T  N  N  S  N  A  P  S  Q  I
```

BUTTON   RIBBON   THREAD
FABRIC   SNAPS
PATTERN   STITCH

Birds of a Feather

Draw some bodies for these bird brains!

Favorite Colors

Find and circle the words in the puzzle.

```
V I O L E T M T G H
N R Y Q Q J C A C E
M E E F C S X A U L
F A Q D K K E P B P
E V U A M P T I W R
I N D I G O D N S U
G R E E N Z D K A P
```

GREEN   PEACH   RED
INDIGO   PINK   VIOLET
MAUVE   PURPLE

Draw a picture of something in your favorite color.

A Tasty Design

Use your imagination to fill in the blanks below. Then, write the words in the story to create your own fun and silly fashion line.

1. Favorite food _____

2. Best friend's name _____

3. Verb _____

4. Adjective _____

For my first fashion show ever, I decided to make dresses out of

_____. It is *not* easy shaping it into a dress! It is also
　　　　1

hard keeping people from eating it. _____
　　　　　　　　　　　　　　　　　　　　　　　　　　2

ate my very first dress! I had to _____ and finish
　　　　　　　　　　　　　　　　　　3

the rest of my line before my show. People are going to love my

_____ dresses!
　　　4

Answer Key

5

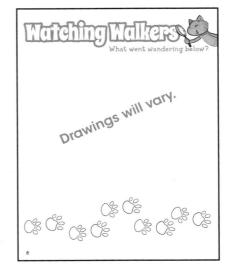

6

7

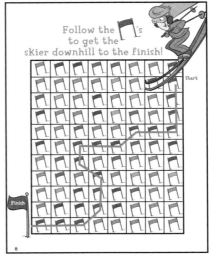

8

9

10

Answer Key

11

12

13

15

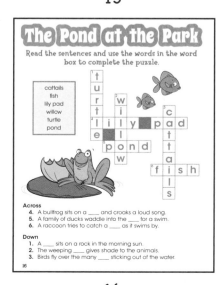

16

17

Answer Key

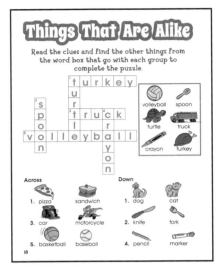

18

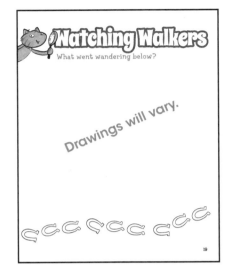

19

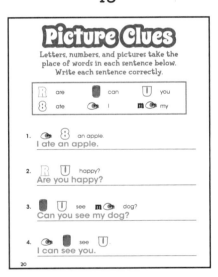

20

21

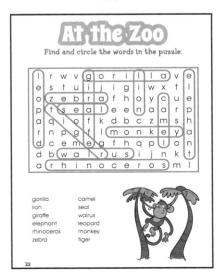

22

23

Answer Key

24

25

26

28

29

30

Answer Key

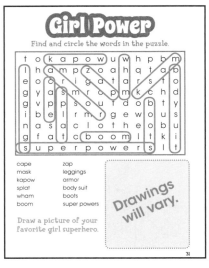

31

32

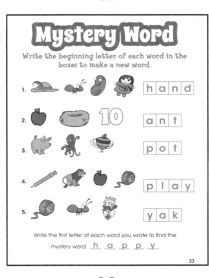

33

34

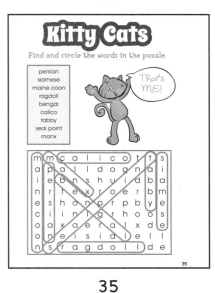

35

36

Answer Key

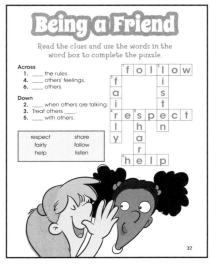

37

38

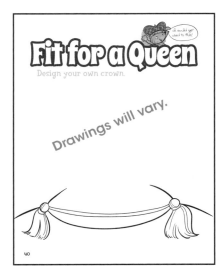

40

41

42

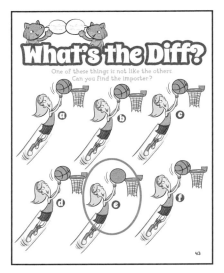

43

Answer Key

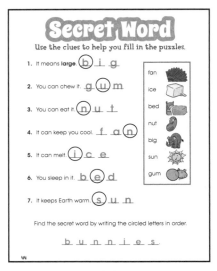

44

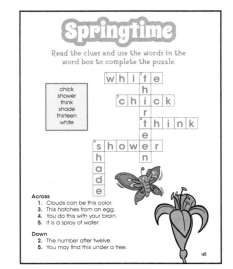

45

46

47

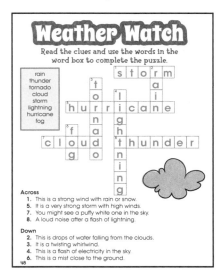

48

49

Answer Key

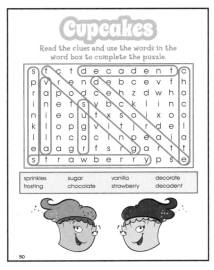

50

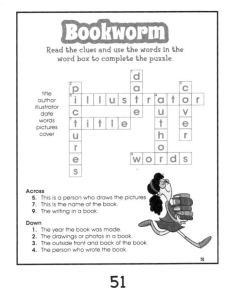

51

53

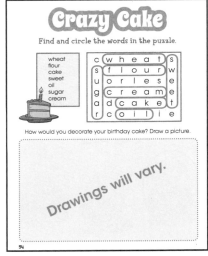

54

55

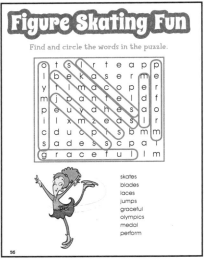

56

Answer Key

57

58

59

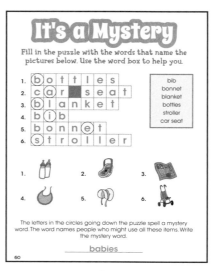

60

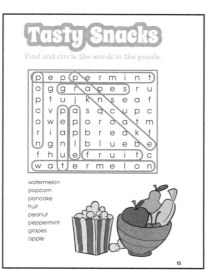

61

62

Answer Key

63

64

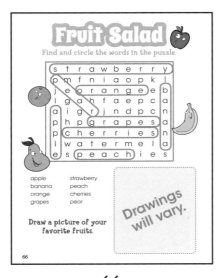

66

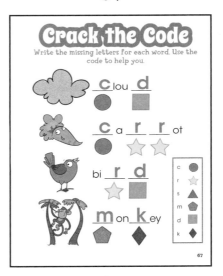

67

68

69

Answer Key

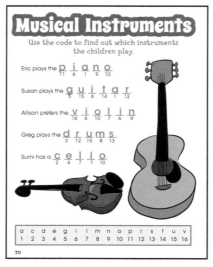

70

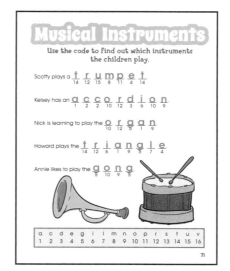

71

72

73

74

75

Answer Key

76

78

79

80

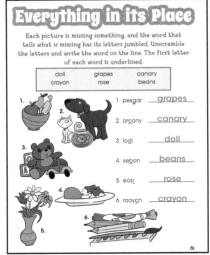

81

82

Answer Key

83

84

85

86

87

Answer Key

89

90

91

92

93

Answer Key

94

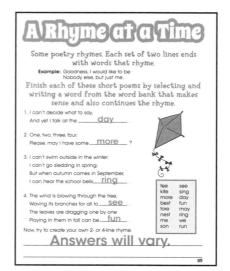

95

96

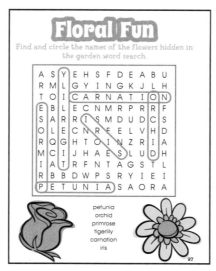

97

98

Answer Key

99

100

102

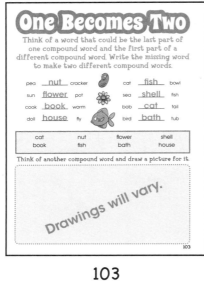

103

104

Answer Key

105

106

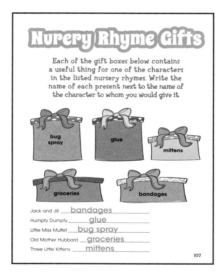

107

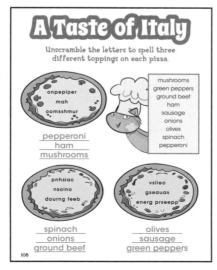

108

109

Answer Key

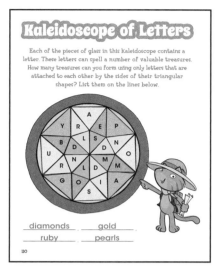

110

111

113

114

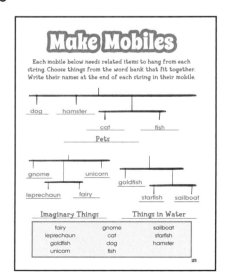

115

Answer Key

116

117

118

119

120

Answer Key

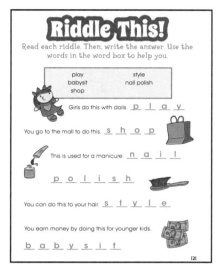

121

122

123

124

126

Answer Key

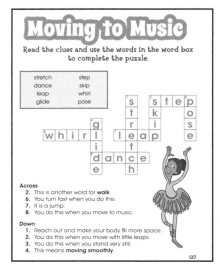

127

128

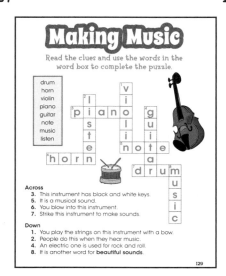

129

130

131

Answer Key

132

133

134

136

137

Answer Key

138

139

140

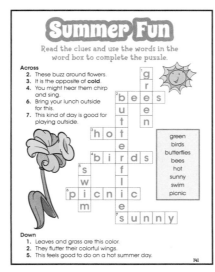

141

142

Answer Key

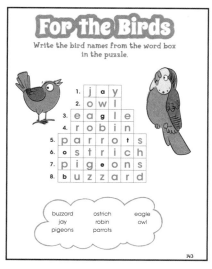

143

144

146

147

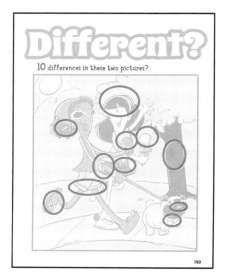

149

Answer Key

150

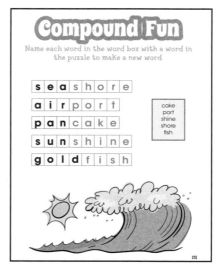

151

152

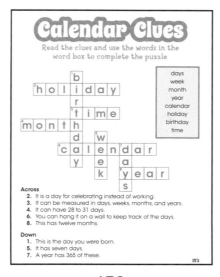

153

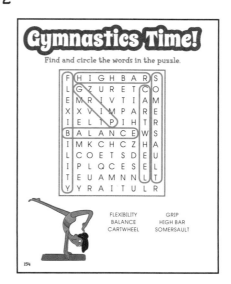

154

Answer Key

155

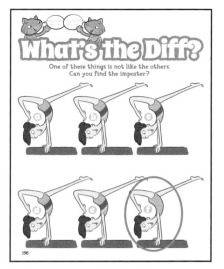

156

157

158

160

Answer Key

161

162

163

164

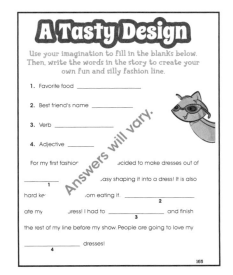

165